D1637002

What It Is, Is Golf

What It Is, Is Golf

TEXT AND DRAWINGS BY

Joe James

New York: A. S. Barnes and Co., Inc.
London: Thomas Yoseloff Ltd.

© 1965 by A. S. Barnes and Co., Inc.
Library of Congress Catalogue Card Number: 65-11696

A. S. Barnes and Company, Inc.
8 East 36th Street
New York 16, New York

Thomas Yoseloff, Ltd
18 Charing Cross Road
London W.C. 2, England

6255
Printed in the United States of America

FOREword

Lots of books have been written about how to *play* golf. No one has bothered to write about something far more urgently needed — how to understand golf *and* the golfers. Both take some real understanding.

Outsiders wonder what the golfers are doing out there — and the golfers also wonder what they are doing out there. A million times every Saturday morning a golfer somewhere lunges at a ball, knocks it a few dribbling feet, and cries out in anguish, "What the !*!*@! am I doing out here anyway?"

But they go stumbling on. This book will explain what they stumble over, what they hit at, why they hit at it, and what they hit at it with. It will also delve into the fascinating history of this crazy game. And it will meet the challenge head-on and probe with a l-o-n-g needle — which takes some real doing.

So come along with us as we scurry through sand traps, around ferocious hazards, and down dog legs in an intense and pixillated pursuit of the red-faced, sweaty-backed golfers and this crazy game called golf!

CONTENTS

FOREword 5
This Is a Golfer 9
This Is a Golf Ball 14
This Is a Tee 20
The Green, What It Is 24
The Fairway, What It Is 27
The Rough, What It Is 29
This Is a Sand Trap 31
This Is a Golf Club 36
Hazards, What They Are 42
This Is a Golfer's Shoe 46
This Is a Golf Bag 48
The Lesson, What It Is 50
This Is a Golf Cart 57
Par, What It Is 60
The "Somes" of Golf 62
How to Understand Golf Tournaments 64
Golfomania, and What to Do for a Victim 69
How to Understand Golfer Talk 74
The Benefits of Golf 77
Lines Written to Close a Book On 80

THIS IS A GOLFER

A golfer is anyone with a club, a ball, and boundless optimism. In fact a true golfer does not need a club or a ball. He can borrow the former and pick up the latter. But no one can be a golfer without optimism. Even though stymied by a dense forest or waist deep in grass burrs, the true golfer is ever hopeful. Somehow, he expects his next shot to ricochet through the trees, or leap out of the grass burrs, and soar dead to the pin.

There are many kinds of golfers. The most numerous are the red-faced hackers, or sweaty backed species, the sclaffer or weak-wristed grass cutters, the burry ankled rough dwellers, and the purple-veined club throwers. The scratch species or solid hitter is almost extinct.

The term "golfer" is derived from Norse mythology. Goff the Hard-headed, son of Look-Up the Elder, was a young man of little talent but great endurance and hope. When the King announced a gruelling contest to pick a husband for his homely but filthy-rich daughter, Goff the Hard-headed was first in line. The rules of the contest were simple. The King had ceramic objects set up in thick brambles, quagmire infested marshes, and along steep gorges and sand pits. The first man to break one hundred of these objects would win the daughter's hand.

A fast running and sure-swinging Pro on the summer tour won the daughter's hand. Goff, bloody and bruised but ever hopeful, was intrigued by the challenge. Even with the Princess married and out of it, Goff went back week after week to plunge through the brambles and sand pits, still trying to break one hundred of the ceramic objects. Little wonder those who followed him, all desperately trying to break a hundred, came to be called *Goffers* or *Golfers* as they are known today.

The first man to break 100 of these ceramic objects would win the Princess' hand.

Today's Goffer, or golfer, is a creature of strangely contrasting make-up. He will fret all week long in anticipation of his Saturday golf game. He will approach the first tee in gay spirits and high anticipation. Three strokes later he is ready to go home.

Away from the course, the game is simplicity itself. Any golfer off the course can tell you exactly how to make any shot. Over a cup of coffee, he can mentally play the course as well as any Pro. But over a golf ball he is suddenly brought back to stark, icy reality, and he usually wishes he were back over the cup of coffee.

Many who take up the game find it a confusing one. In most games, tennis for instance, the object is to get in as much play as possible. In golf the object is to play as *little* as possible. The worst golfer is the one who plays the *most* in any given round. Other golfers will urge him to take lessons, so he can play *less* each round. It is puzzling that so many who supposedly play golf for exercise strive to reduce the amount of exercise they can get from any given round.

In golf, the trophies always go to the golfer who plays the least. *This is all wrong.*

And it is indeed reassuring that the vast majority of golfers resist this "do as little as possible" philosophy. In the true spirit that built America, they refuse to hold back or accept the minimum as a goal. They ignore the cunning terms designed to induce minimum performance like "par shooter," "low eighty golfer" and similar terms. Instead, they strive to get as much exercise and get in as many strokes per game as possible. These are the true red blooded golfers, and they enjoy an overwhelming majority. The "do as little as possible" golfers, while in the minority, do control the rules committee, score card printing, and also manage news releases that keep heaping praise on the golfer who uses as few strokes as possible.

Some happy day they'll change things and the trophy will go to the fellow who takes the most *strokes in any tournament.*

But some day the true golfer will come into his own. Then the perfect golfer will no longer be the fellow who gets around the course in the fewest strokes. It will no longer be the fellow in white shoes, unsoiled slacks and immaculate shirt with not a trace of under-arm stain. Instead, the perfect golfer will be a red faced, sweaty character covered with grass, burrs, and an occasional wood tick. And gentleman that he is, he will carefully kick the mud off his soggy shoes before he strides up to receive the championship trophy for taking the *most* strokes in the tournament.

That will be a great and wonderful day and we, as thousands of other high-scoring golfers, can hardly wait.

THIS IS A GOLF BALL

Golf balls are hard-covered, dimpled spheres that cost anywhere from five cents to $1.75. The main difference is that the $1.75 balls will disappear even when on a fairway, and they simply will not float. A ten cent ball will skip right across a pond and land on dry ground. It is rarely picked up in a fairway.

The price of a golf ball is usually based on two things: compression, and mark-up. Pros hit a high compression ball with a hard cover. For the hackers they recommend a lower compression ball with a softer cover. This seems backwards since the soft covered balls cut up pretty easily. However, this does keep golf ball sales (if you'll pardon the expression) rolling.

Some golf balls have a professional golfer's name printed on them. Buying these is risky business. Any day you may be playing golf, getting ready to hit one of your $1.75 pro-name balls, when someone taps you on the shoulder.

You look up and here is this Pro and he says, "Pardon me, but you are about to hit *my* ball. See, it has *my name* printed on it!"

So you stand there speechless while this famous, well-known pro picks up the ball and walks away. If you have other balls readily visible with his name on them, he would be within his rights to take them also. You are much wiser to play with a lower status golf ball like an Amoeba 3 or a Barnacle XXX.

But by all means do have a reputable Pro examine the golf balls you play with. Do this especially if you are having problems with any phase of your game. You may discover, and only a Pro can tell you, that you are playing with *left-handed* balls.

So you stand there speechless while this famous well-known pro picks up the ball and walks away. If you have any other balls visible with his name on them, he would be within his rights to take them also!

The title to a golf ball is a fleeting thing. Newcomers to the game do not realize this and often cannot understand it. One fellow who had obviously just taken up the game came up to the Pro shop counter. "I just finished playing the first nine holes," he explained, "and I believe I lost my brand new Amoeba 3 ball on the ninth fairway. If somebody turns it in, will you please save it for me? I'll come back after we finish eighteen." The Pro, a kindly man, took the fellow into the back of the shop and privately and soothingly explained the facts of golf and especially golf balls.

Research has proven time and again that golf balls have a higher turnover by far than any other item. If the government could make dollars circulate as well and change owners as frequently as golf balls, business would always be booming. At any given club or course, all golf balls are owned by *all* the players at least once every thirty days. This does not exclude balls lost in water hazards. These are salvaged by skin divers or deep breathing little boys and re-sold to the Pro shop, which in turn re-sells the balls to the golfers. It is a system as beautifully balanced as any found in nature. The older, wealthier but weak-eyed golfers can afford new golf balls more often. They are preyed on, politely of course, by the younger sharper-eyed golfers who find any ball that has stopped rolling.

If you intend to acquire balls in this manner, you must, of course, use discretion. Otherwise you will find that the golf course is truly a splendid place to meet new people.

Just when a golf ball is "lost" is a point of great importance. Precedent is usually taken from the case of O'Reilly *vs.* Sullivan, the State of New York, 1887. This now famous case decided once and for all that ownership of a golf ball remains with the original owner even after the ball has come to rest. O'Reilly's tee shot landed in the open ball pocket on Sullivan's golf bag. Sullivan claimed the ball was his to have and to hold since it reposed among his golf balls. The Judge ruled otherwise. "Sure, and had Sullivan found yer ball and placed it in his golf bag, it would truly be his," the judge ruled. "But since it *flew* into the bag and the acquisition was not of Sullivan's doing, then the ball still belongs to O'Reilly."

"We ain't lost our ball yet. We are still looking for it!"

You will hear many so-called rules about how long a golfer is allowed to look for a ball that has been lost. We waited some fifteen minutes while a twosome up ahead hunted for a lost ball. At long last we walked up to where the two guys were poking the bushes. "Look fellows," we explained, "there is a rule that players hunting for a lost ball should let the foursome behind play through."

"Oh, we know all about that rule," one of the golfers replied, "And we will certainly obey that rule. Only we ain't *lost* our ball yet. We are still *looking* for it!"

When you buy new golf balls, and eventually even the sharpest eyed and most nimble golfer has to buy new balls, watch how the old timers buy golf balls. A novice

will hold the new ball belly high, drop it on a concrete floor or sidewalk, and see how high it bounces. He will, acting extremely wise, select the ball with the highest bounce for the least money. An experienced golfer will never do this. Instead, he will place the prospective ball on a smooth, level table or counter and then watch it closely for at least a minute. If the ball *moves,* he will not buy it. Experienced golfers know that almost all inferior golf balls, in some unexplained manner, move just before you can hit them. So by careful examination, they eliminate these balls. If you doubt this, watch an experienced golfer who uses carefully selected balls. He takes a slow back swing and does not hurry his swing. He is not the least concerned that the ball may move before he can hit it. But novices, not as careful in selecting balls, are plagued with the kind of ball that invariably moves before you can hit it. Their only hope is to hit the ball quickly, before it moves.

So examine balls carefully before you buy them. If you still have trouble hitting the ball properly, have the club Pro check you out. If he cannot help you, see your doctor. Your doctor may discover, after weighing you, that you have been hitting the ball too fat.

That about covers the points you should know about golf balls. And of course golf balls are not absolutely essential. A man at our course discovered he could save money, and much frustration, if he did not use a golf ball. He simply *imagined* he had a ball teed up and took it from there. All of us envied him because he was the only guy who came in week after week in good spirits after eighteen holes. In fact, another golfer was so captivated by this fellow's unusual game that he joined him. They played a twosome each week with nary a ball in sight. They moved briskly along the fairway, happily chatting and never missing a shot. They were truly the perfect golf twosome until they began betting. In no time the bet had grown to a $1,000 and they approached the final hole deadlocked. We watched them from the club house as they came jauntily down the final fairway. Each took his turn, swinging smoothly and crisply at an imaginary ball. Then suddenly one threw down his club and charged the other. They were clobbering one another furiously as we raced from the clubhouse and pulled them apart.

"What happened, what happened?" we demanded. "What happened to spoil such a perfect, happy game?"

"We were going fine," one snorted, wiping a bloody nose, "and it was all even on the bet. Then this !*!@*! character played *my* ball!"

So while you do not really need a golf ball to play golf, using one does help to pin each golfer down to reality.

THIS IS A TEE

A tee is a small wooden pedestal. It is so small that it is actually *teeny*. And that is where the tee got its name.

Many things about golf are confusing and contradictory. The term "tee" is one of these. Although the tee is a tiny wooden pedestal no longer than your little finger, you will frequently hear a golfer say, "We are next on the tee." This is confusing. Not even one golfer, much less four, can get on one tee. In this case the golfer is speaking of a different kind of tee. He refers to the tee box, which is really not a box at all. In fact, there are rarely any tees around a tee box. We'll let you ponder that while we get back to the matter of the tee.

Golfers carry tees so they can place the ball on one before hitting. Legally this should be done only when hitting from the tee box. Some golfers, always the good ones, frown on teeing up balls in the rough. But most golfers, always the bad ones, will tee up a ball anywhere. They will tee up a ball in the tall grass or even in a sand trap if they can do it without being seen. Shifting a ball to a tee requires great skill and lack of moral fibre. The shifting of a ball to a tee actually brought about the word *shift-tee* or *shifty* as we know it today.

Some pros will tell you the tee is the only gadget ever invented that really helps the golfer. Such comments are a low blow to the maufacturers of swing groovers, hip-unlockers, head-keeper-downers, and elbow-holder-inners. But wooden tees, though sorely needed for a long time, are a rather recent invention.

Before tees were created, golfers used little mounds of sand. Each golfer carried a pocket full of sand. When it was time to hit a drive, the golfer took a small handful of sand from his pocket and made a little mound of sand. Then he placed the ball on it and smacked it with his driver. This was called "sanding up" the ball. The "sanding up" area was not called a tee box in those days. It was called a "sand box."

When golfers came home after a round of golf, they scattered sand everywhere. Their wives complained bitterly, and, for a few nerve-wracking years, golf teetered on the brink of extinction. It was at that precise moment that some inventor should have rushed forward with the wooden tee. But instead, inventors went right on sweating over less useful things like television and jet airliners. The golf course operators, sensing that a pocket full of sand was about to put them out of business, hurried to correct the situation. They dumped loads of sand at convenient spots around the golf course. Now golfers no longer need to carry sand in their pockets.

But the move, designed to help the golfers, boomeranged badly. Many shots strayed into the piles of sand. Conscientious red-blooded golfers, though in the minority, insisted on knocking the ball out of the sand. Getting out was such an exhilarating experience that the rule makers and course designers were delighted. "We can make the game even more interesting," they exclaimed, "if we place sand piles at tricky places around the course — places where we can trap the unsuspecting golfer." And thus, because of the need for a tee, the sand trap was born.

Today golfers' pockets are usually full of tees instead of sand. But a pocket full of tees is still a hazard. Tees should be carried in the front pockets, but never in the hip pockets for obvious reasons. Golfers who fail to do this and sit down suddenly frequently tee themselves up!

THE GREEN, WHAT IT IS

The green is a smooth grassy place where all golfers in any foursome eventually get back together again. The green always has a flag stuck on it somewhere. The object is for the golfer to knock his ball into the hole this flag is stuck in. This is called "putting out," although it is obviously "putting in."

Some people think the "green" got its name from the color of the grass or from the color of golfers' faces as they leave the putting area. Neither is true.

The primitive days of golf coincided with the primitive days of medicine. Any wound might well be fatal due to infection. Golfers who had to go into the rough were often attacked by local marauders or hostile invaders from the mainland. It is true the golfers carried weapons right along with their primitive clubs, but the hostiles wisely waited until the golfer was on his back swing. Then they charged in. Many golfers were killed outright. Others were severely wounded but, like true golfers, would not quit because of a mere hacked up arm or leg. They played on, in spite of their wounds. By the time they had reached the putting surface, gangrene had often set in. So it was logical that golfers of those days, seeing so many of their buddies stagger up to the putting area with gangrenous wounds, called the area the "*gangrene*" place. This was later shortened to "green."

Many severely wounded golfers played on in spite of their wounds. By the time they had reached the putting surface, gangrene had often set in.

Greens usually require great care. Most golf clubs have a man who takes care of the greens. He is called a "greens-*keeper*." But in many cases he lets the greens get away.

Greenskeepers work through the week, However, a standard rule around most courses is that the greens must be mowed only on Saturday morning and watered immediately thereafter on Saturday afternoon. If this were done during the week when few golfers are on the course, not many would realize how much care the course receives. But since it is done on Saturday when the course is teeming with players, vast numbers see first-hand that the course is receiving the very best of attention and care.

"There goes our pin setter now!"

Greenskeepers receive few kind words and lots of blame. They have little chance to get even. Now and then a greenskeeper, fed up with criticism and griping, will go berserk. He will sneak out to the course, hide behind bushes near a green, and when a golfer eventually sends a shot a foot or two from the pin, the greenskeeper will sneak from his hiding place and quickly move the pin some thirty feet away.

Most greenskeepers never go this far. They are content to wait until a golfer is hunched over a birdie putt and then fire up their mower. Or they will set water sprinklers on the greens and, hiding nearby, chuckle delightedly while golfers try to run in and putt without getting soaked.

In any event, greens are an important part of the game of golf. They give the game some of its most exciting moments — and most colorful language.

THE FAIRWAY, WHAT IT IS

The fairway is a little used portion of the golf course. It extends from in front of the teeing-off area to the green. The fairway is usually flanked on both sides by higher grass — and golfers.

The word "fairway" originated in the early days of golf. The areas on both sides of the playing area were permitted to grow wild. Golfers in this undergrowth area could sneakily throw their balls to a better place to hit from, tee them up, or engage in other shennanigans to hoodwink their opponents. But once a golfer got in the closely mowed area, his every movement could be clearly watched by his opponents. He had to play the fairway without cheating, so the term came to apply to the portion of the course where every movement, even a gentle nudging of the ball with the club, is clearly visible. It is the area where you have to play *fair*.

Some fairways follow a straight line from the tee to the green. Others are said to "dog leg" right or left. These picturesque terms also originated in the early days of golf. Golfers in those days played under trying conditions with wild animals and often blood-thirsty brigands lurking in the rough along each side of the fairway. So golfers trained dogs to follow the ball and retrieve it from the dangerous rough if necessary.

It was logical that, when the fairway turned to the right, the dog would have to "leg it to the right" to follow the ball. If the fairway had a bend in it, golfers would say "Here's where your dog legs to the right," or "Here's where your dog legs to the left."

THE ROUGH, WHAT IT IS

The *rough* is the booger-land or scary area that laps up against each side of the fairway. The fairway is kept well-watered and mowed, but in spite of all this care, most golfers prefer to play in the rough. They are always over there in the unmowed grass. This is probably because the rough offers more challenge than the fairway. Balls are difficult to see. This adds suspense and an element of the chase. An occasional snake, now and then poisonous, adds a pinch of danger.

It is not known for sure how the term "rough" originated. Chances are good, though, that it was developed in Scotland in the early days of the game. There were no mowers as we know them today. Peasants hacked out the fairways with scythes. The areas on each side of the fairways were too rough to cut with scythes. Game was abundant here and the golfer who pursued his ball off the fairway was quite likely to flush a covey of ruff grouse with his thrashing swings. When someone asked, "Where is Mac" a member of the foursome would yell, "He's off there swinging in the ruff grouse." Logically, "grouse" was dropped as the quantity of game diminished, and today we merely say, "Old Mac is out there in the ruff," or *rough,* as it is now spelled.

Many courses take pride in their carefully cultivated "rough" and develop strains of horrible briary-like weeds and grass to harass golfers. Golfers describe these courses with awe. One golfer recently, telling of an especially horrible course, explained "I'll tell you how rough that course is. I lost four balls in the *ball washer!*"

Probably the world's most horrible roughs fringe courses in Africa. These courses are located adjacent to game preserves, and wild animals frequently roam near the fairways. They are not allowed *on* the fairways but do lurk in the rough. Golfers stay together for protection, and the local people all wisely hit short and straight shots down the fairway. Visitors, amazed that they can out-drive the short-knocking locals, brashly go all out. For a time these visitors may eat up the course. Then it is vice versa. When an experienced local golfer gets in this horrendous rough, he always tells his caddy to bring a nine-iron *and* the rifle. These courses are also known for their slow greens and quick sands. Obviously, most of the regular players on these courses are steady players who score well. The more erratic ones are culled out by the wild animals or eaten by the cannibals.

THIS IS A SAND TRAP

A sand trap is a scary place filled with squishy loose sand and surrounded by high banks and leering golfers.

For most golfers a sand trap is a frightening place to be. The man who invented the sand trap probably got the inspiration while watching ants fall into the sand traps made by doodle bugs, or "ant lions," as the more learned call them. The doodle bug excavates a funnel-shaped pit in the sand and then hides at the bottom. The ant who tumbles in scrambles frantically to get out while the doodle bug flips up showers of sand to keep knocking the ant down. A few ants escape, but usually the doodle bug eventually gets a solid grip on a leg, and that ends it for the ant. A golfer in a sand trap is in much the same situation. He tries repeatedly to get out of a sand trap and each time is showered with spurts of sand. The only difference is that he eventually escapes and goes stumbling on to other sand traps.

A few golfers have no fear whatever of sand traps. Some even aim for the traps. Pros do this if they have a tough bouncy green to shoot at or a dangerous hazard behind the green. At least one duffer we know also does this. "If I hit into a trap," he explains, "the chances are better that nobody will steal my ball. And if they do steal it, they leave *tracks!*"

The man who invented the sand trap probably got the inspiration watching ants fall into the traps made by doodle bugs, or ant lions.

Sand traps are sometimes called "cat boxes" or "the beach." They are also called other things. One golfer, after years of frustration from sand traps, specified in his will that he be cremated. He requested that his ashes be then taken to a golf course and small portions dumped into each sand trap on the course. "I want to get even," he explained, "by personally frustrating other golfers for years and years."

The Pros brush off a shot from a trap as casually as you would brush off so much sand. They make the proper shot by hitting one, two, or three inches *behind* the ball. Us weekend golfers get it *almost* right — we hit one, two, or three *times* behind the ball.

On almost any beach during the summer months you are likely to see some guy in a bathing suit swinging a sand wedge. "I vowed to master sand trap shots during our two weeks vacation here at the beach," he will probably tell you. And sure enough, after a week or so the guy can hit out of sand better than any Pro. But when he gets back on a golf course after his two week lay-off, he has forgotten how to hit all the shots *except* the sand trap shot. And, as you probably guessed, he hacks wildly around the course but *never* gets into a single sand trap!

The rules about playing from sand traps are very strict. You are not supposed to touch the ball before you hit it. You are also not supposed to touch the sand with your club until you swing. If you are especially fast, you can innocently ask, "Are we playing winter rules?" and then, before anyone can stop you, blithely tee up your ball on a lump of sand with your club head. A few golfers who were willing to practice at great length have perfected sand trap techniques that are beautiful to see. As they

approach the trap, they palm a second ball. Then, entering the trap, they covertly step on the ball in play and stomp it deep into the sand. Taking careful aim at an imaginary ball, they swing smoothly and, at the proper moment, release the extra ball. The palmed ball pitches gently to the pin and, now and then, actually goes in. This technique must be used only when you are away from the other players or when your opponents are weak-eyed.

After hitting, slashing, or clubbing your way out of a sand trap, you are supposed to carefully smooth the sand for the next fellow. Many long-time golfers do this smoothing bit from habit. One Pro, during a nationally televised tournament, plunked his ball onto a sand bar in a water hazard. He removed his shoes, waded out, and smacked the ball off the sand bar. Then, while millions watched, he methodically smoothed the mud with his club, leaving the sand bar unblemished for the next golfer who might stray in.

Good sand trap technique.

"That little guy can't make the shot either!"

Some golfers take a sand trap in philosophical stride. If they cannot get out of one, they suffer quietly. One we know took seven or eight swings and watched the ball roll back into the deep trap each time. Then he noticed a doodle bug busily excavating his own tiny sand trap in the bigger sand trap. He watched it a moment, fascinated by the sand being flipped up by the doodle bug and then remarked, "That little guy can't make this shot either!"

THIS IS A GOLF CLUB

A golf club is a device a golfer uses to club at a ball. The lower end of a golf club has a flat area for hitting at the ball. The handle, or shaft, tapers upward to meet the golfer. The portion of the handle nearest the golfer is the broader or fattest part. The portion of the golfer nearest the handle is likewise.

Golf clubs are called *woods* and *irons*. The woods in early days were made out of crude, gnarled sticks. Golfers were not very accurate, and when they teed up the ball for a drive, often said, "Well, here's one that's likely to go in the woods." So logically the clubs were called "the woods."

When metal-headed clubs were added, golfers did not do much better. Instead of hitting down on the ball, they tried to scoop it just as they do today. The result, then and now, is a dribble or a shank or a bladed ball. Any time a

The portion of the handle nearest the golfer is the broader or fattest part. The portion of the golfer nearest the handle is likewise.

golfer reached for his metal-headed club in those early days golfers gave him plenty of room. They knew he might "get his ire up" and throw the club. These clubs became so strongly associated with violent temper that they were at first called the "ire" clubs or "ire-'uns." Later this was shortened to "irons."

Golf clubs are all numbered. This is a great aid to the golfer and can be readily explained. The higher the number on the club, the shorter distance it will knock the ball. An 8-iron will knock the ball about 125-yards. A 5-iron should knock it about 155 yards. A 1-wood, or driver, should knock the ball 250-yards. But the 1-wood is a very versatile club and is also used to make little short dribbly shots off the first tee. In fact it is used primarily on the first tee by most golfers and then rarely after that.

When you think about it the "1" on the "1-wood" may well mean "use only on the Number 1 tee."

The distance obtained from a golf club varies with the golfer. The golfer who, aided by a good bounce, can get 125-yards with an 8-iron always feels an inner cringe when he reads that some 14-year-old has scored a hole-in-one "using an 8-iron for the 150-yard par three hole."

Golf clubs are important for more than just hitting at the ball. They offer the golfer many alibis. Clubs, for example, change with age. A golfer whose clubs knock the ball great distances when he is twenty will often discover, twenty years later, that the clubs have lost a great deal of the zing they had before. This is why most golfers get rid of their old clubs every few years.

An entire book could be written about putters. Putters are probably the only clubs that come close to having human qualities. A putter can be undependable, mean, and completely aloof to pain and suffering. Then, the next day, the same putter can be warm, helpful, and truly the best friend you ever had. Putters get very little credit for anything. When a golfer had a good round, he says "*I* putted well today!" But when he has a bad round, he growls, "My !*@!* putter was awful today. I might as well have been putting with a !*!@!* rattlesnake!"

Many golf clubs on the market are named for famous golfers, but you will find only a very few putters named for well-known golfers. This is probably because putters are so undependable. Few well-known golfers want to let their name be put on such an erratic club. You can well imagine how you would feel if you were a well-known Pro named George Schmoe, and you heard a golfer shout, "Missed another !*@!* three foot putt! This blankety-blank *George Schmoe* putter is for the birds!"

The other golf clubs are generally more dependable, so the Pros readily let their names be used on these clubs. Many present-day Pros have clubs named for them. Few people, though, remember that famous golfer of years ago — McDaniel A. Dirty. But if you check on any golf course, you will find most of the players today are playing with *Dirty* clubs.

You will find very few putters named for well-known golfers. This is because few well-known golfers want their name put on such an erratic club.

That about covers the main points you should know about golf clubs. And this information can be most helpful to you. One wealthy Texas oil man had never bothered to learn the intricate details about golf clubs as we have outlined them for you here. A friend did a nice favor for this Texan and the oil man wanted to repay him. "Forget it," the friend insisted. "It was nothing at all!"

"But I want to do something nice for you," the oil man persisted. "I want to buy you something you need but wouldn't buy for yourself. What do you need?"

"All right," the friend finally gave in. "I could use some golf clubs."

"Fine, fine," the oil man smiled. "And how many do you want?"

"Oh, the regulation number will be fine," the friend said. "That's fourteen clubs."

A year went by and the friend assumed the oil man had forgotten completely. But one day the oil man looked him up. "Well," he began happily, "I'll bet you thought I'd forgotten about them golf clubs!"

"Frankly, I had forgotten about them myself," the friend admitted. "Like I said, you needn't go to the trouble. What I did for you was something I enjoyed doing. You don't have to give me anything."

"Oh but I did!" the oil man beamed. "I rounded up them fourteen golf clubs for you. Reason it took me so long is I couldn't find that many for sale at one time. But I finally rounded up the fourteenth golf club for you last week and bought it. It is not quite as nice as the other thirteen — ain't got no swimming pool — but it is still a mighty nice golf club."

HAZARDS, WHAT THEY ARE

In addition to other golfers, there are many hazards on a golf course. Hazards are scary places designers have worked into the course to trap careless or unskilled golfers.

The term "hazard" came from a half-lizard sort of monster that lived for many years near the golf course at Loch Ness, Scotland. Golfers who strayed from the open fairways were devoured by this monster. When a golfer failed to reappear, it became routine for the other golfers to say, "He must be in the Hazard."

The good golfers paid little attention to the Hazard. After all, the Hazard never came out on the fairway to devour golfers. A shy creature, it was at first content to lurk in the rough or scary places. But eventually, after eating all the clumsy golfers around Loch Ness, hunger forced the Hazard to come out on the fairways after the better ones. That was too much, and the king called out the army and drove the Hazard into Loch Ness lagoon.

Today "hazards," while less ferocious, are an integral part of any golf course layout. A hazard is anything on the course that gets the golfer into difficulty. This may be a water hole, a ditch, or the golfer's big mouth.

Water hazards serve two purposes. They add excitement for the golfer who must hit over them. They also

Water hazards serve two purposes. They add excitement, and they also help keep the Pro Shop supplied with used balls.

help to keep the Pro shop supplied with used balls. A ball knocked into a water hazard costs you two strokes. In addition, it costs you the ball.

During a nationally televised tournament, one Pro carefully studied his ball as it lay in a shallow water hazard. He decided he could knock it out of the water and save that extra stroke penalty. While millions watched on television, he sat down and carefully removed his left shoe and sock. Then, his mind entirely on the difficult shot, he stepped into the water with the *other* foot.

Water that has gathered on a golf course after a rain is called "casual" water. If your ball falls into this, you rake it out without charging yourself a stroke. Many golfers conclude that other water, in the hazards, got there the same way, so they "casually" rake their ball out and do not count the stroke. Blows sometimes follow, and this is where the term "casualty" came from.

He carefully removed his left shoe and sock and then, while millions watched, stepped into the water with the other *foot.*

Golfers in the northern part of the country have a definite winter-time advantage over southern golfers. Water holes freeze over. Golfers who dare the icy weather — and many do — can retrieve balls from the ice. Some even play off the ice.

At one northern club a stranger asked the Pro if he might play the course. The Pro put the stranger with a local threesome of hardy winter golfers. This threesome did not relish having a newcomer thrust on them. The weather was cold, but the reception the stranger got was even colder.

On the sixth hole the stranger knocked his ball onto a water hazard. "Onto" is correct because the hazard was covered by a thick sheet of ice. Gingerly the stranger eased out on the ice and recovered his ball. He saw more balls farther out, abandoned by other golfers who were afraid to go out on the thin ice. A little guy, the stranger gingerly eased farther out and recovered several nice new balls. He tossed these back to his companions with his compliments. Suddenly the ice cracked and the stranger fell in.

His companions rushed to his aid. They formed a human chain to save him, then built a fire to dry his clothes and thaw him out. Then, with the stranger dry, they continued the game — on a much pleasanter note. Telling about it later, the stranger said, "Those guys were not very friendly at first, but they turned out to be pretty nice fellows after I finally broke the ice."

Some ditches on a course are not considered hazards. If you get in one of these, you are permitted to drop out. But others are hazards, and if you get in one of them, you have to knock the ball out. If you hack away until you drop, your friends are permitted to carry *you* out. This is called a "free lift."

That covers the main hazards you are likely to meet on a golf course. One should mention a slightly different type of hazard you may encounter — a stranger with an unknown handicap. And one final hazard that should be mentioned is a green located near a highway or busy street. This is one of the most dangerous of all hazards, especially on weekdays. Your boss may drive by and see you playing.

Suddenly the ice cracked and the stranger fell in. His companions formed a human chain to save him.

THIS IS A GOLFER'S SHOE

When playing golf, a firm and solid footing is essential. Early-day golfers played without shoes, digging their toes firmly into the turf to keep from slipping as they swung. Playing without shoes called for great accuracy since the golfer who got off the fairway would get his feet full of burrs. (This was where the term *burr-footed* originated.)

For years golfers played burr-footed — that is, without shoes — and strove to stay in the area fairly free of burrs — the fairway, as they called it. Then, in 1872, Clete McNamara, a poor but ingenious cobbler, took up the game of golf. Clete, who made his living making shoes,

rebelled at playing burr-footed. "We canna have so many fellers playin' wi'out shoes," Clete proclaimed. "It is bad for the bloody cobblers." To give shoes more grip, Clete drove his cobbler nails through the soles but did not bend them over. Clete's shoes caught on fast. A vast market of burr-footed golfers pounced on the idea. Today most golf shoes have modified versions of Clete's nails, or *cleats* as they are now called.

Cleats on golf shoes prevent slipping, give a golfer a firm footing when throwing a club, and make a rugged masculine *clompety clomp* in the club house.

In rainy weather cleats can be a problem. They pick up mud badly. Some golfers have learned a simple way to get rid of mud on cleats. They give a lusty forward kick like a punter or a girl in a chorus line. The mud will go sailing thirty yards or more. Never do this toward a water hazard. Your shoe may fly right with the mud and, thanks to Clete's cleats, will sink immediately.

THIS IS A GOLF BAG

Some beginning golfers think a golf bag is a female version of a golf bum. This is not true. The golf bag usually contains golf balls, tees, insect repellent, ball retriever, cigarettes, a rules book, often a fifth of scotch (for scotch foursomes), lighter, spare jacket, golf glove, pencils, umbrella and, of course, golf clubs.

Most golf bags are bought by wives. When a husband casually mentions that he is thinking about taking up golf, his wife goes into action on the next birthday, anniversary, or Father's Day. She does this not knowing a golf club from a tee. "He needs a nice bag," she will tell the department store clerk. "Something he can carry with brown or white golf shoes and that goes well with brown, or gray, or blue slacks. Perhaps you have something in a Koret or Lewis bag, with shoulder strap." When a smart department store clerk sees one of these lady prospects approaching, he usually slips a pocket mirror into one of the more expensive bags. That always helps get a quick sale.

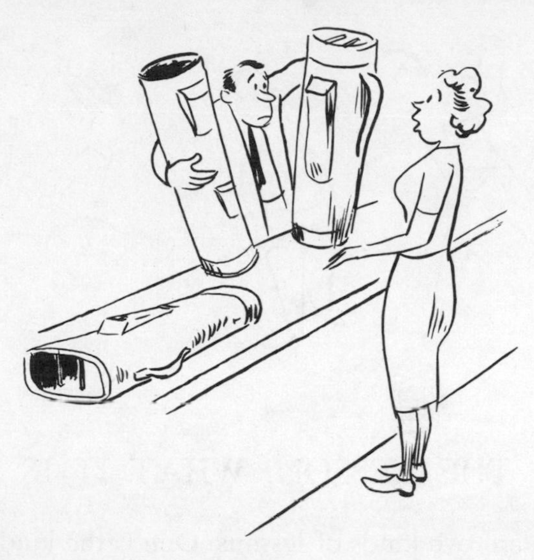

"I think he would like something he can carry with brown or white golf shoes . . ."

All types of golf bags arc available. There are bags made of leather, canvas, plastic, mink, lizard skin and alligator. There are bags with seats attached, bags with ash trays, hooch compartments, transistor radios, one man life rafts, and even bags that fold into a bed. You can always tell when a golfer has bought his own bag. It is a light canvas affair.

THE LESSON, WHAT IT IS

There are two kinds of lessons. One is the kind you ask for and pay for. The other is the kind you do not ask for but get anyway.

Lessons you pay for usually consist of instruction given by a professional teacher. But a few grossly egotistical week-end hackers have charged their neighbors or relatives for, to use the term loosely, "instruction." Usually these hackers "charge" for instruction in other ways than money. The guy they're helping learn the game may say, "I'll buy the beer because you are helping me to learn to play golf." Or "Use my edger," or "No need to pay me back for the sack of charcoal briquets you borrowed. After all, you are learning me to play golf."

Nothing makes a true-blue golfer sicker than to see some fellow who has just received a set of golf clubs taking lessons from a neighbor — and all because the neighbor got his clubs a week earlier and now knows the game. At such sights, Pros will squirm in agony, and some will cry like babies. When a "teacher" doesn't know — and doesn't know he doesn't know — his students are in for massive frustration.

The urge to teach is in us all. We do not need a teacher's certificate to begin. At a driving range one recent evening, an obvious beginner was getting a lesson from a friend. The friend gave explicit instructions and caustically criticized the beginner's errors. But the "instructor" never once took the club to demonstrate. He was too smart for that. A short time later the "teacher" was gone and the beginner was now busy giving instruction to another newcomer!

"Nothing personal, but you are not hitting the ball clean."

Now and then a hacker "instructor" does pass out some sound advice. At a Houston driving range not too far from the space project, a scientist was watching a co-worker hit at balls. Time and again the co-worker's club smacked the earth first, then hit the ball with a dull scuffing "splat." The scientist counselled, "I say, old boy, but I do believe you are hitting the *larger* ball first!"

In teaching golf, just as in teaching anything, there is a real need for good communications. The instructor may be talking about one thing while the student thinks he means something entirely different. A typical example of this was the Pro who watched his student scuff shot after shot and finally said, "You are not hitting the ball *clean!*"

"I am too," the student replied in a hurt tone. "I had a shower this morning!"

A lesson from a Pro is a different thing again, in a way. For while a hacker is usually eager to give instruction, some Pros have to be literally forced to give lessons. They may need the money, but they're reluctant to let outsiders in on the real game. In fact this reluctant or aloof air is common around many Pro shops. You get the feeling that this is a Sanctum Sanctorium — the private lair of a fortunate and select little group who feel their golf know-how sets them apart from the oafs who come in to spend money. When they take your money it is with an air of revulsion, as though they are selling the lodge secrets down the river a little bit at a time. One well-known Pro was constantly pestered by a hacker. "I'm having great trouble with my drives," the hacker told him. "Please show me how to hit a drive."

The Pro put him off as long as he could and finally agreed to show the hacker how to hit a drive for one hundred dollars. The hacker plunked down the hundred dollars, and the Pro, famed for his booming drives and fluid swing, took the hacker out to the practice tee. The hacker started to tee up a ball, but the Pro stopped him.

"Nope," said the Pro. "Just stand over there and I will show you how to hit a drive." Then he methodically teed up three balls and sent each one screaming down the fairway. Turning to the hacker he said, "Now that is how you hit a !*@!* drive!" and walked back to the Pro shop with the hacker's hundred dollars in his pocket.

Perhaps this low appraisal of Pro shop sales ability comes from a recent experience. A friend reminded the head Pro that he really should stock some of "this fellow's humorous golf books." "Golfers will buy 'em," he stressed. "They're a perfect gift for a golfer. . . . And you can make a nice profit on 'em. Wouldn't cost you a cent if you didn't sell 'em."

The Pro hesitated. My friend went on emphasizing the profit angle. "They don't cost much," he added. "And us guys at this plush joint don't mind spending money. Look how many of us pay $4.50 for a glove even when it has half the fingers cut off!"

The Pro smiled and weakened. "Okay," he said. "Those books sound pretty good. Send me *three*."

Now and then you meet a Pro who is a real salesman, a fine instructor, and a warm logical fellow who is quick to say, "Golf is a game any person with normal physical equipment can learn to play well if he has the time and the desire to practice." This especially applies to any Pro who has bought this book.

Pros will tell you most lessons follow pretty much the same pattern. The golfer tells his "trouble" to the Pro and then proceeds to analyze the cause of the trouble himself. When the Pro starts to give an opinion, the golfer will pop in with "You know, *I* noticed that and I figured it might be what was causing my trouble." Sometimes the Pro may get one or two good shots out of the golfer, and that may satisfy the student that progress has been made. Often though the Pro will shake his head and say, "This is gonna take a lotta time to unlearn what you been doing." And the golfer will nod and agree he has been a Number 1 dolt. A golf lesson from a good Pro is 35 per cent practice balls and 65 per cent tees and sympathy. A psychiatrist's couch should be on hand for most lessons and probably will be any day now.

Some really sharp golfers have learned that "instruction" can be a massive weapon in any match. Wisely these guys will not offer instruction unless it is asked for. Even good golfers will sometimes mutter, "I wish I knew what I'm doing wrong." That is all the invitation these torpedoing teachers need.

"Well, since you asked me," one will say gently, "you are picking up your left heel too much."

"Oh, am I?" the other guy will exclaim. "Well, by golly! That is why I have been topping them. Thanks a lot. I know how to correct that!" And correct it he does. But he concentrates so much on keeping that heel smack on the ground that the rest of his swing collapses.

Corrective suggestions can be "lack of wrist break"; "too much wrist break"; "hitting off the right foot"; "not watching your back swing"; "watching your backswing"; "moving around too much"; "not moving around enough," and so on. Any of these, mentioned casually, can hypnotize a golfer and turn him into a frustrated hacker for four hours at least.

A lesson may also be "indirect." If an opponent is playing well you may casually mention, "I have finally figured out what has been wrong with my swing. Saw an article by George Schmoe this morning and he says 90 per cent of the trouble comes from lifting the left heel (or not lifting the left heel) and boy has it helped me!"

No matter how good your friend is playing, that will haunt him. Soon he will try lifting his left heel (or holding it down), and right then you have him in your pocket.

So you see, the "lesson" can be many things. It depends entirely on *who* is giving it.

Lessons, example 1: Some students require close personal attention and supervision.

Lessons, example 2: Other students do better without close supervision.

THIS IS A GOLF CART

Golf is a game people play for exercise, and golf carts are powered carts they ride in to get less of it.

Some golfers drive carts much better than they drive golf balls. In fact they seem to get more genuine pleasure from driving the cart than from playing golf. They are in a constant dither to be back in the cart and away. Many a golfer, about to putt, has heard the skidding of tires and looked up to see a golf cart and four beady eyes. To be in a walking foursome and have two cart loads of impatient golfers behind you is much like walking across a long railroad trestle with the train due any minute.

Our little foursome was moving along at a prettty good clip for walkers when we heard a yell behind us. "Mind if I hit?" Back on the last tee was a still-throbbing cart and a vibrating golfer teeing up a ball. "Just a minute," we yelled back, "till we get out of range." Then the guy

hit, and banged his ball into a ditch forty yards in front of the tee. He leaped into the cart, roared to the ditch, left it still rolling to get at his ball, and, with club held high, yelled, "Mind if I hit?" There was nothing to do but give him lots of room. He reached the green in a flurry of clubs, three-putted in the blink of an eye, leaped back into his cart, and roared away. We watched him with great distrust. At his speed, he would probably be coming back through on his second eighteen holes in a matter of minutes, and might even go into some sort of golfing orbit.

If you must ride a cart, leave your wallet at home, or keep your pocket solidly buttoned. Hopping in and out of a cart will pop your wallet out of your pocket. If you do lose your wallet, go back over the course as quickly as you can and mentally re-play every shot. You may not find your wallet, but you will play the round much better than you did before.

There are many kinds of carts. Some are gasoline driven. Some are electric. Carts usually run well for the first ten holes. If anything is going to go wrong with a cart, it always happens when you are farthest from the club house.

On the course, never leave your cart unattended with other golfers nearby. Some wise guy may disconnect a wire and hover nearby while you try to start the cart. When you finally give up and walk away carrying your clubs, he will replace the wire and blithely use your cart for the rest of his round.

Modern carts were designed after considerable study and, as a result, can foul up from many causes. Typical happenings that can put you afoot three miles from the club house with two eighty-pound golf bags are: (1) a battery that suddenly goes limp, (2) a drive belt that breaks, (3) a starter that quits working, (4) a fender that comes unbolted and locks a wheel, and (5) a brake that will not release. A friend of ours was quite the stuff with a new push-button drive cart he had rented: That is, until something went wrong with the push-button hook up. The cart would not go forward. It would only go *backward*. He finished the round driving the cart backward and steering it by sitting on the front of the cart and facing the rear.

Carts are driven at some golf courses in such numbers that traffic signs are posted along the course. "Slow down here," or "dangerous curve." Every now and then some golfer is clobbered when his cart overturns. A friend of ours said, "Stop here . . . be fine," and stuck out his leg to get out of the cart. His buddy didn't hear him, didn't stop, and the leg caught. It shattered in two places. The doctor who set the leg, a great believer in exercise, said, "This is what you get for putting the cart before the course!"

PAR, WHAT IT IS

Golf is an odd game, and so are the terms connected with it. If you try to understand the word "par," which golfers toss around a great deal, you may as well brace yourself for more confusion.

Par applied to golf means the "normal or average amount of strokes" required for a certain hole — or for the entire course. This is a confused and misleading statement in itself. If you *averaged* the scores for all golfers on any given course, par would more likely be 108 instead of 72. So where did they come up with the delusion that 72 is average, or par?

As you probably guessed, par is actually an abbreviation for "*par*anoia". And paranoia, as you well know, means a "mental derangement — especially a chronic form of insanity characterized by elaborate delusions." Any golfer, as he walks up to the tee on a given hole, sincerely *thinks* he can par it. He thinks this even if he took a *fourteen* on the preceding hole. Ninety per cent of all golfers are engaged in this eternal and frustrating attempt to equal par. The other ten per cent have given up.

There is another strange quirk about par. Few golfers shoot par on a given course this week. But last week many did it. The amount of golfers equalling par increases in direct proportion to the amount of time since a game was played. This is known as the *law of diminishing returns.*

Non-golfers have adapted the term "par" and given it equally warped usage. A doctor may take a patient's temperature and say, "Well, you've got 102 degrees of temperature. How do you feel?" And the patient will say, "Below par, Doc." Any golfer will tell you 102 is not even close to par. The patient should correctly say, "Doc, I feel lousy. Way *above* par!"

Confusing, to be sure, but so is the game of golf.

Par is actually an abbreviation of "paranoia," *which means* "*a mental derangement characterized by elaborate delusions.*"

THE "SOMES" OF GOLF

Many newcomers or non-players are confused and puzzled by the "somes" in golf. There is no need for this as we will explain.

Probably the most frequent "some" is the four*some*. A foursome consists of four players who tee off together.

A two*some* consists of two players and is not very popular on Saturdays. Twosomes must be very patient. They have to wait all the time.

A one*some* is usually an individual with B.O. or some other annoying character trait, like winning all the time, who must play alone because no one will play with him. Onesomes score better than other "somes" since no one else is watching. They spend much of their time waiting for the other "somes" to get off the green.

A onesome is usually an individual with B.O. or some other annoying character trait like winning all the time.

A slow-playing group that loses at least one ball a hole, dallies too long on the tee, and takes too long on the putting green is called a "gruesome."

A three*some* is a twosome that has added a onesome. Or, often, a threesome is a foursome in which one member is no longer speaking to the other three. Foursomes usually become threesomes when one member is *caught* cheating on his score. There is nothing wrong with cheating on your score in golf. The crime or sin is to get caught at it.

Other "somes" are five*somes*, six*somes*, and seven*somes*. Five somes and sixsomes are permitted on week days. A fivesome is pretty slow — about as slow as a feminine twosome. The term "seven*some*" is rarely used. In most cases, more than five golfers are called a "gang*some*."

This covers most of the "somes" in golf except one. This last group is a slow-playing group of any size that loses at least one ball on every hole, dallies too long on the tee discussing the last hole, takes forever to get off the putting green, and usually forgets to put the flag back up. This group is called a "grue*some*."

HOW TO UNDERSTAND GOLF TOURNAMENTS

"Tournament" comes from medieval times. In those days knights from all over the realm gathered to see who was the best of all. There was gaudy raiment, loud talking in the press tent, and considerable complaining during practice jousts about how the field was mowed too short, too long, or not mowed at all.

At a given signal the knights charged at one another, and they kept at it until all but one had been knocked off

The winner received a sack of shekels. The losers packed their battered armor, muttered "wait until next week," and headed for the next tournament. It is the same way with golf tournaments.

his horse. The survivor or winner received a sack of shekels and a special coat of mail with the local tournament crest emblazoned on it. The losers packed their battered armor, muttered "wait until next week" and headed for the next tournament. It is the same way with golf tournaments.

When you go to your first golf tournament, it is well to study the people first before you start watching the golfers. You will notice that most of the folks have little tags tied to their shirts or blouses. They are such avid fans that they are likely to forget where they came from. These tags have that information. You will notice others wearing special bands on their arms or hats labelled "Marshall."

In the early days of golf in America, a movement got under way to have the game outlawed. Then a Chief Justice of the Supreme Court named Marshall wrote a blistering opinion, which stopped the movement and helped get golf securely rooted in the U.S.A. As a tribute, anyone named Marshall today is admitted free to any golf tournament. Be nice to these people. Even if they did not pay to get in, they are due respect.

You will notice that not more than three Pros play together during a tournament. This is one of the faults of golf tournaments. It would be much better if all Pros in the tournament, usually about fifty of them, teed off on the same hole at the same time. They could play it, then move on to the next hole. The gallery could then watch all the golfers at once. Many more cold drinks could be sold while the fifty golfers sorted their balls on the green. There would be far more color and activity. Instead of three stone-faced Pros striding methodically up the fairway, fifty anxious golfers would converge on a ball-splattered green. There would also be far more suspense. With fifty golfers putting in succession, it would take some time to find out who won the hole.

You will notice at tournaments that when the Pros walk onto the putting green the crowd does not follow. This is another phase of the game that should be corrected. It is rude. The gallery should never shun golfers. Some of the more sensitive Pros may feel the crowd is avoiding them because they need a shower. But after walking for nine holes or so, most of the gallery can usually use a shower also.

If you are out there following the Pros during a tournament, go right out on the green with them. This makes them feel welcome. You will also notice that the Pros, out there alone on the green, frequently misjudge the break of the green or how fast the ball will roll. Go out and give them some advice and help, especially if you have played the course before. It is the least you can do. If one of the

Marshalls approaches, brush him off. And if he gives you any static, tell him your name is Marshall too, but they didn't have a "Marshall" hat your size.

You will notice caddies carrying sticks with cards on them saying things like "1 under," "even," or "seven over." This card is a report on how the players are playing. "One under" means that one of the players has gone under for the third time and is not likely to come up. He's out of it. "Even" means nobody is mad — the players are all *even*-tempered at this point in the game. "Seven over" means one of the players would like to go back and play the seventh hole over. Permission to do this is seldom granted.

Whenever a Pro finishes the final hole in a tournament, you will notice he always goes into a little tent. Some Pros go in this little tent to check and sign their score cards. Others go in there to be sick.

After the tournament is over, it is time for the awards. Tournament officials are never content to give the winner a check for $15,000 and a huge cumbersome cup. They also want to put a coat on him. The coat is emblazoned with the tournament crest, just as in days of old. It is always a coat, never a coat and pants. And the puzzling thing about the ceremony is that the jacket always fits as though tailor-made. How this is done is a well-kept secret. More than likely each Pro carries an "award" jacket in his luggage. If he wins, a tournament official sneaks into the locker room, tacks a crest on the jacket, and hurries back with it. Then the golfer's own jacket is slipped on him and the crowd exclaims, "My, how nicely it fits!" or "Just like it was tailor-made!"

That just about covers the things you would want to know about tournaments — except possibly how to watch one on television. And on television, with cameras lurking in trees and on towers high over the players, you know just about everything that is going on. Except, perhaps. when they are going to sneak in a commercial.

GOLFOMANIA, AND WHAT TO DO FOR A VICTIM

A majority of golfers, thank goodness, can play the game onc or two afternoons a week and leave it alone the other five days. A few weak characters, normal in every other way, simply do not have the will power. Golf becomes a driving obsession with them. Only early home-therapy or thorough psychiatric treatment can save them.

The symptoms are easy to recognize. The man on the verge of becoming a *par*anoic or golf addict will not quit when the other fellows have played eighteen holes. He goes on for twenty-seven or even thirty-six, staggering home long after dark, a gasping, red-eyed, sweaty hulk. He hides putters around the house or stashes drivers in secluded places outside the house. Even when his clubs are taken away, he covertly grips imaginary club handles. Waiting for a bus, he will absent-mindedly drop into a putting stance and stroke an imaginary ball.

Jobs have been lost and families torn asunder because a father became a golf addict. The best treatment is to sense the problem early. Many times an understanding wife heads off disaster by building a putting green in the back yard. This is hard work for a woman. Other wives take up the game themselves and then can get in brief visits with their husbands while waiting to tee off or before starting the second eighteen holes.

One wife tried these home therapy methods with no luck whatever. Her husband was slipping deeper and deeper into golf addiction. She saw him seldom, even in the winter months, and then only when his buddies brought him home frozen stiff. In desperation she talked him into consulting a psychiatrist.

She went with him to the first psychiatrist they consulted. Later she would regret that she did not go with him into the consulting room. Each week the husband came home from his "treatment" in great spirits. He was always anxious to go back, but his golf addiction was as severe as ever. Curious to see what the treatments were like, the wife stayed out in the waiting room for twenty minutes or so one day, and then slipped quietly into the consultation room. Her husband was lying on the couch. The psychiatrist was putting at a glass.

Her husband was lying on the couch. The psychiatrist was putting at a glass.

"Twenty dollars an hour you charge us," the wife yelled, "and you putt at a glass while *my husband* is on the couch!"

"It's fair, dear," the husband explained. "When he misses, *he* has to lie on the couch and *I* get to putt!"

The second psychiatrist she took him to see was a non-golfer. In fact, he detested the game.

The second psychiatrist examined the golf addict husband at great length. He gave him truth serum and learned only that the patient should have been turning in scores in the high nineties instead of the low eighties. But this did not get at the basic problem.

It was only when the psychiatrist tried "flash cards" with various design arrangements that he stumbled on the real problem.

He showed the harried patient a card with two triangles. "What are these?" the psychiatrist asked gently.

"Them's two *tees,*" the patient explained happily. "Two guys is getting ready to tee off."

The psychiatrist flashed a card with a simple square on it.

"That's a *tee* box!" the patient responded.

Next, a card with a large circle and a smaller circle inside of that. "Somebody just holed out a putt!" the patient reasoned.

Then the psychiatrist extracted a card with a weird, involved design. A huge basin-like outline covered most of the card. Inside it were squares, triangles, rectangles,

and many tiny circles. "And what is that?" the psychiatrist asked hopefully.

The patient thought a long time. "Well, it looks like a huge lake."

"Excellent, excellent," the psychiatrist beamed, "and what are the other objects?"

"That square thing is a sunken box," the patient went on, "and those smaller rectangle-shaped things are beer cans lying on their sides. That's an old tire . . ."

"Excellent, excellent . . ." the psychiatrist nodded.

"And," the patient finished, "all them little round things at the bottom are golf balls. That's a !*@!* water hazard!"

By that time the psychiatrist knew he had a tough case. "This will take some extended treatment," he told the patient. "You are far too involved in golf. *Everything* reminds you of golf. It dominates your very life. It is at the root of all your problems. But I can help you. Come back next Monday at two P.M."

When the patient got home, his wife was pleased to learn the psychiatrist had offered hope. "I know he will help you," she smiled and added, "By the way, dear, I invited some folks over to play bridge tonight."

"Fine, fine," her husband responded, already a much cheerier fellow.

"That's wonderful," his wife replied. "You never wanted to play bridge before. I'm so glad you went to see this second psychiatrist. And one more thing, dear. We need another couple for tonight. Do you know a couple — perhaps somebody new — we might invite to fill out?"

The husband brightened. "Say, that *psychiatrist!* He is a delightful fellow. And he's bound to have a charming wife. How about inviting them?"

His wife agreed that would be a fine idea. "Call him," she urged.

The psychiatrist was most receptive. "My wife and I will be delighted to attend the bridge party," he said. "And thank you so much for the invitation."

Then the husband had a sudden thought. "By the way, Doc," he added. "When you come, how about bringing all your dandy *golf* pictures?"

HOW TO UNDERSTAND GOLFER TALK

Golfers speak a language all their own, and theirs is a language as strange and perplexing as the game itself.

The lingo of the game is important, and lack of it quickly marks the novice. If you say, "Well, I *boogered* that hole," your companions will quickly know you are a novice. So if you are just taking up the game, learn to understand and use the correct lingo. After all, the game is 75 per cent talk. So let's check into a few typical terms golfers use.

Hit inside-out. This is the panacea to end all golfing troubles. Unless you are doing this, you are not playing golf. It means simply that the swing must start inside the line of flight and finish outside. This prevents slicing. Any golfer will be glad to show you what this means with a beautiful inside-out practice swing. Then, when he hits a ball, he will swing outside-in.

Reading the break. This is a bit of lingo to describe the process of oggling a green from a squatting position in an attempt to predict which way a putted ball will roll. It can be a simple squat, squint, and putt procedure, or it can be an involved ritual more complicated than a rain dance. Most golfers who try to read greens do not get the message.

Strong wrist action. Any golfer who out-drives the fellow doing the talking has "strong wrist action." in case a husband is striving for this attribute, his wife can help him get it by letting him clip hedges and edge the yard.

Follow-through. At the end of any match, the winning golfer is supposed to follow through and buy drinks for the losers. If he fails to do this, he has poor follow through.

Greens are fast. This means the golfer has been missing his putts.

Greens are slow. This means the golfer has been missing his putts.

The rough needs mowing. This means the golfer has spent very little time on the fairways.

The fairways need mowing. Another way of telling someone you are a pretty darn good golfer and spend a lot of time in the fairways.

The course is in excellent shape. This means, "I shot way over my head today."

The course is in horrible shape. This means, "I played my usual lousy game today. Shot a hundred and twelve."

"I shoot 'bogey golf'." This means the fellow shoots 90 and is afraid to shoot better than that because he might lose his job.

A scratch golfer. This is a fellow whose game is so good his friends are just *itching* to replace him in the foursome.

In addition to a language all their own, golfers can also communicate in what seems like grunts and shrugs. They are all suffering in common and converse in a hodge podge, but readily understood mumble of words. Here is a typical example:

Howjado?

Nahbad. Haddanatey ate.

Goodiniswind. Wuzzacoursecrowded?

Nah! Fewduffersout annabunchawimmen.

I hatewimmenona course. Theyletchaplay thru?

Nah! Aggravatinashell.

Greensfass today?

Nah! Slow annalottabrake.

Yerputtsdroptoday?

Yeh! Droppedinna twennfootbirdie puttonnate.

Assgrate. Well, we're nextonnatee. Seeyaround.

Okay. Hiddumstrate anseeyaround.

THE BENEFITS OF GOLF

Golf offers many benefits in addition to the mere enjoyment of the game. It builds character. If you investigate, you will find more characters around a golf course than just about anywhere.

Golf also develops many latent or hidden talents. As one acquires skill in golf he also acquires other skills he never dreamed were within him.

One skill golf frequently develops is the ability to design. A pro golfer who never stitched a button on a shirt can win a big one and suddenly reveal a talent for designing golf slacks. What is more, even though these are the first pair of slacks he ever designed, a firm is ready and willing to risk large sums of money on this golfer's creation. Other designers, waiting patiently but hopelessly in manufacturers' reception rooms, have much to learn. If they want to design slacks, they should first learn how to play golf and play it well.

Golf also develops clothes sense and good grooming. A golfer may have the poorest clothes sense on the tour. Before he hits the big time, he may play day after day in ill-fitting black pants, plain white shirts, and muckledydun and dirty shoes. But if he suddenly begins to win

A golfer may dress like an unmade bed. But let him develop golfing skill, win a few tournaments, and you'll suddenly see him in a full-color ad with his clothes fitting like a glove!

some big ones, his taste develops right along with his skill. You may have marvelled before how one guy could look so much like an unmade bed. But now, seeing him in a full color ad, you are delighted to see that his clothes fit like a glove, that colors match, and that the big pot he formerly sported is *gone*. It is indeed amazing how developing golfing skill also develops clothes sense and good grooming.

Golf develops discriminating taste too. For years a golfer struggling on the tour will be content to smoke anybody's cigarettes. But let him win several big tournaments and, lo and behold, he develops such an acute and discriminating taste that he will smoke only *one* brand of cigarette. And he feels so strongly about it that he goes on television coast-to-coast to tell one and all of his amazing discovery.

Golf also brings latent or little-known skills or knowledge to the foreground. Golfers who never fixed a flat in their lives can win a big tournament and suddenly, literally overnight, discover they are skilled judges of good automotive design.

Golf helps you develop warmness and an interest in other people. Take the golfer on the tour who never had time to speak to other people. They were just so many geese around the green. They were just so many noisy characters to be put up with on the course and avoided elsewhere. But let this golfer start winning some big ones and a marvelous change takes place in his personality. He is suddenly a changed man. He takes time to speak to people and to be keenly interested in their problems. He may even pause to recommend a better hair oil or shaving lotion.

So if you lack good taste, or if you yearn to design anything from sports jackets to ear muffs, take up golf. You will be surprised and delighted how the game will bring out your hidden talents.

LINES WRITTEN TO CLOSE A BOOK ON

Yes, Golf is a slightly daffy game.
You chase a little ball.
You whack away with an odd-shaped club
That is no help at all!

You pursue the ball oer rock and hill,
Thru heat or icy cold.
This mad passion grips the tender youth
As surely as the old!

Why such fools pursue the little ball
Is a mystery to me
Perhaps you *can fathom it, my friend.*
I'm *next up on the tee!*